I0182168

Burn

Burn

by

Kathleen Johnson

WOODLEY PRESS

Copyright 2008 by Kathleen Johnson
All rights reserved
Printed in the United States of America

Library of Congress Control Number: 2008930719

ISBN: 0-939391-45-7-X

WOODLEY PRESS
Washburn University
1700 SW College Ave.
Topeka, Kansas 66621

Edited by Kevin Rabas
Cover painting *Legacy of Light* by Louis Copt
Book design by Pam LeRow
Printed by Lightning Source
First printing, 2008

Contact Kathleen Johnson at:
johnsonvkathleen@hotmail.com

For Michael,
Jarrett, and Lauren

Table of Contents

I. An Ember under the Deepening Ash of Days

II. By Fitful Campfire Light

III. Searching for a Spark

When we want everything to change we call on fire.

Gaston Bachelard,
The Psychoanalysis of Fire

I

An Ember under the Deepening Ash of Days

Rise and Fall

Here I stand
in the Colosseum, all
cleavage and smiles, dazed

by ghosts of gladiators,
dazed by ungodly sun.
It's Rome, August,

in this photo you snapped
a few months before
our marriage. How

could I, at twenty, know
the future, the past,
where all roads finally

lead, how moonless nights
would find me, decades later,
in this dusty Kansas town

in a house of arches,
feeling the heat of history
bearing down?

Controlled Burn

Late winter dusk.
Land undulates
like the smooth curves
of a woman as they drive through
the Flint Hills on the way to
somewhere else. Gray highway
under gray sky. Earth dun-colored,
denuded. He steers in silence, wants
no music. She has nothing
to say. They're on the way
to somewhere else. She feels
numb: a blank canvas, a white sheet
of paper, a treeless expanse.
Soon, spring will come,
and with it so much
will go up in smoke.
Like these hills,
she hungers for fire.

Eclipse

The first time you called
your voice passed over me
cool as a shadow.

Mosaic

I want to make
the intricate tessellated moments of our lives
a floor of jade, obsidian, turquoise, ebony, lapis.

Arthur Sze, "The Moment of Creation"

Winter

Corelli's *Christmas Concerto*, chocolate and oranges in a sunny chair,
red scent of cinnamon, colors chasing like children
through December air. A new year promised to open, open
as a stained-glass window might, if it could, a passage to salvation. Then
the year turned; so did he. Future fell silent, a diamond ring into snow.
He left and took the colors with him. Even my dog's white fur felt cold.
Raw winds whipped and moaned. Nothing to do but try to hold on.
It was the time of violet shadows. Violet, color of the end of the known
and beginning of the unknown. A twilight world. I could have wandered
into a picture on my wall, say Brueghel's *Hunters in the Snow*,
followed those lean dogs of winter wherever they might lead. Anything
but the gray procession of days and dread, endless walks down gravel roads.
Where is your God now? Hope is a hard, hard stone.
January's moon rises, a broken piece of milky quartz. Opaque. Cold.

Spring

Colors gradually resurrect themselves after weeks of fathomless blue.
Opalescent sunrise, sliver of ghostly moon. Even the darkest hues
are something to hold onto. I hear polished obsidian in Bach's *Ciaccona*,
onyx thunderheads in the voices of the *Carmina Burana*. I've given up
on God and promises. Colors speak to me: forsythia branches
arranged in a silver vase, jellybeans in a jar. Redbud trees
emerge in the woods. Their green hearts shimmer, orchid branches reach out

like arms. This world is more than the sum of its parts. I wear a ring
with a sapphire star and fill the house with hyacinths.
I plant rosemary and try not to remember. By April, green and new
are the same syllable. The word for him doesn't exist. Sudden storms
stir winds of change. I walk in woods of malachite, emerald, peridot.
And red still burns at the opening and closing of days.
The sun is a blood-red garnet. I won't let go. I'm learning a new language.

Summer

Hours fan out like mammoth sunflower petals.
A wedge of lemon cake waits on an amethyst plate.
Afternoons linger long and late. Color is its own language,
running rampant as I reach for it. Why try to hold on
to what's over? Sunlight escapes into the dark. Iridescence gathers:
dragonflies around a murky lake. Instead of gold-flecked midnight,
this silent bedroom, that full moon harsh as an interrogation light.
One definition of desire, always waiting for what never came: two
palettes combining, incandescent days. Nothing prepared me for evenings
blue as topaz. Turner painted with his brightest red though he knew
it wouldn't last. Van Gogh believed yellow was capable of charming God.
Even tomato vines, the potted basil on the porch, smell of summer's citrine.
There's nothing not stained with color. Across the road,
wildflowers dot a field, brilliant as gemstones.

Fall

He said it's all about letting go and then he did.
After the shatter, I keep stepping on the brilliant, the hard, the sharp.
Nothing is clear anymore. My world turns colors, so many shades
between creation and destruction, between loss and gain.
So many scattered pieces of love and hate. All year I wait
for autumn, but gold days pass; amber memories burn.
If everything we touch goes, why do we yearn
to hold on? Color is its own language and my only fluency.

Light filters through trees, each ruby leaf
holy, illuminated. Hummingbirds hover between
fading lantana blossoms. A heron flies in mist over the pond.
Bees buzz in thyme and lavender. Bluestem blows in the wind.
A shooting star streaks across black sky, leaving
a magenta and cobalt question mark, briefly, above us all.

Love

means nothing.
Even the word itself is vacant.
See how that capital *L* forms only half
a frame. It can't hold
anything. And the *o*,
so completely hollow.
The *v* throws empty arms up
into vast white space.
And the little *e* curls into
itself, at the end, alone.

Double Portrait

(After Seurat's *A Sunday Afternoon on the Island of La Grande Jatte*)

Sitting here on beach rocks,
we're just two bodies,
unmoving shapes on a shore
of silt and rubble, two voices lost
in the weak surf. If anyone were listening
they'd hear our voices
losing. Waves advance
and retreat but do not wash us. Nothing
washes over what is
over. Time won't allow it. It gives
only distant cries of seagulls,
an owl's call high above
the space of an afternoon, wide blue
we'll never escape into.
If Seurat were painting this scene,
he would do it in beads of blood.

Still Life in February

I sweep my hand across your face,
a faded photo, you as a boy. Gone.
Dreamless sleep. Your hands
not touching me. Bach instead
of Al Green. Gifts I don't receive.
Jokes I can't recall. Not hearing
the phone ring. Gray days thinning
to dust. Gravel on a road.
Ice glazing windows. Waking up cold.
Every word I never said.
The whole earth holding its breath.

Portent

The night you arrived:
northern lights shimmering red
in black winter sky.

Bloomsday

shall I wear a red yes and how he kissed me under the Moorish wall
and I thought well as well him as another . . .

James Joyce, *Ulysses*, Molly's soliloquy

Yes well Molly got it wrong it's never many men or just any man always
only one like it's just this one June day as relentless sun burns as we head
into the open golden throat of summer roadside daylilies shout in orange
what blooms today is gone tomorrow therein lies the rub the tale the
one that lasts much longer than a day the one that ends when I do in the
distance the nervous glitter of a city in fading dusk all these stars fallen
down fireflies flickering around me while Van the man sings everything
that I do reminds me of you and it's true there's this shimmer that wants
to turn into pure gold my daughter in a black bowler at midnight watching
Alex and his droogs while following along in the book it's my *Clockwork
Orange* summer she says later in bed listening to Ludwig van passions
come in deepdown torrents to us both full copper moon through the
skylight so bright I can't sleep keep remembering Billie Holiday's voice
in the car last summer I'll be looking at the moon but I'll be seeing you
O yes so many sultry nights of heat lightning distant thunder but no rain
never any rain the scent of damp grass wild clover on the open window's
breeze wide awake in the dark again silk gown slipping cool over warm
skin soft night air a lover's caress without the lover yes she said whatever
you are seeking is seeking you so much blooms so much stays buried how
to escape from this shadowland of longing how to live in the flat bright
daylight of the real world again someone wrote that desire is a question
that has no answer still I will how can I help it I will offer my Yes.

Subtleties of a Winter Twilight

Evening descends. Here
in the blue shadows of day
colors meld into gray.

Bare limbs sweep the sky.
Deer forage ghost-like
in fields around the house.
A crescent moon rises
with a Cheshire-cat smile.

I sip Merlot,
and my mind melts
like a candle, flickers from
scattered thoughts to your face,
your voice deep as this
darkening night, finally to
what I most want to feel
against December's cold:
your warm breath
on my skin.

So I wait where
there are no hard edges,
my burning
the only light in the window.

February 14

White drifts, white sky, ice
and silence. No one can hear
my red heart beating.

Burn

These shades of desire:
garnets glowing warm around my neck.

Moon on the horizon, a crescent of fire.
The sheen of my stockings as your hand slides up my thigh.
I slip off my heels. You close the door.
A glass of Cabernet left half-empty on the hearth.
My parted lips stained crimson as Eve's apple.
Heat mirage of red, eyelids closed against relentless sun.
An ember under the deepening ash of days, you fanning it again and again.

Rise: A Charm Against Depression

Imagine a radiance.
Crystalline tones against a somber backdrop.
A figure floating up
from the deep.
Palette of sky and sea.
Billowing, boundless.
Looking down, thinking back,
I see you as an absence of color, nothing
but grim negation, dead weight. Me,
I've turned into turquoise sky and water lights.
I feel no pull, no gravity. I've left
your shadow behind, set myself free.
These are incandescent days.
At night, aquamarine dreams
swim in the dark of sleep,
iridescent flashes in a black opal.

II

By Fitful Campfire Light

Frontier Bride

First year of marriage
in a one-room cabin on the prairie,
and for weeks on end it blows—
whirring at the windowsills,
rattling the walls, bending the creek willows,
billowing my skirts. Endless
gusts of wind I hear with each whipstitch,
with every broom sweep,
constant as my own
breath, whimpering around
the doors of my dreams until I want
to slam them shut. Only
sometimes, late at night
with him, a blessed hush,
when—wedding quilt slipped to the floor,
head thrown back, hair a silky tangle,
orange sickle of moon curving
through the window—
I'm lost
in love wild
as an autumn field.

FFA Jacket

My mother lifts
the dusty jacket out of her
cedar chest, hands it to me. I'm surprised
it doesn't smell of liquor: the dark-blue
corduroy jacket with the gold
Future Farmers of America emblem across
the back, his name in gold embroidery
on the left chest, and the title—
National President 1950-51.
I think of the scrapbooks full
of newspaper clippings, pictures of Dad
in this jacket at nineteen, before
college and Korea, poised
behind podiums, posing on tractors,
giving radio interviews, on TV, even tipping
his Stetson on a hometown billboard
that says *Welcome to Freedom.*
A handsome Oklahoma farm boy, the future
of America over fifty years ago. My father,
who now lives far away,
body and mind ruined by booze.
I slip the jacket on
and try to remember
for him. Mom tells me he was always
on his best behavior when
he wore it—"like Ronald Reagan
in the Oval Office," she says, "always
wore a suit and tie, out of respect, you know."
And I wish he'd never taken it off.
I'll keep it, along with his gavel,
all the eight-by-ten glossies,
and the program with the photo
of him presiding over the national convention
in Kansas City—Municipal Auditorium packed
with young men in blue jackets, some of
340,000 members that year, big brass band,
balconies draped with red-white-and-blue

banners and American flags, Dad
sitting in the middle of it all,
looking, as he always has,
so utterly alone.

Farm Wife

In the farmhouse on long
Oklahoma days
she waits
for peaches and tomatoes
to ripen, words
in her head.
Plump love-apples
line two kitchen windows
while she skins peaches.
Velvety curls drop
into a pail, pelting tin
one by one like rain
on the chicken-house roof.

Countless wedges
of angel-food cake
are cut for her husband,
neighbors when they visit,
and the sunburned strangers
who help with the wheat harvest.

Each Saturday,
wearing a dress, dark lipstick,
she drives red-dirt roads
into town to sell
her cardboard cartons
of fresh eggs.

And twice a week
she waters her multitude
of houseplants—African
violets, begonias, wandering
Jew, the tall rubber plants,
and grape ivy—while
poems lie in her
bureau drawer
and jars with handwritten labels
collect dust
in the dark fruit cellar.

Grandad Scott

To this day
his name conjures a scene
I replay as if it's an old black-and-white film:
in the clearing where chickens feed
the air is still, sultry-warm.
Suddenly, out of nowhere,
an immense bird whirls down at me
from sky dark with thunderheads.
It swoops close.
Wings rasp like grain shaking into a silo.
Dirt and gravel scatter
as I run to clutch his striped overalls,
eyes aimed at his work boots.
I'm afraid to look up.
When I turn loose
there's only a far-off speck wheeling away
in sullen sky,
my grandfather roaring with laughter
because I'm a city kid afraid
of a chicken hawk.

When my brother was still a toddler,
Grandad sat him on top of his tallest tractor.
Even above the engine's deafening rumble
he could hear the two-year-old's
terrified screams. That
was Grandad's idea of fun.

That, and naming cows after
his daughters-in-law.

One afternoon
on the front porch of the farmhouse,
he told us grandkids how surprised he was
that Uncle Franklin had grown up
to be a policeman. He'd always thought Franklin
was the biggest sissy of all his four sons.

Back in 1949,
when their small town held a banquet
for my father, who was elected
national president of FFA, Grandad waited
until Grandma finished getting dressed,
then refused to go with her.
I imagine her at the bureau mirror,
silent, unclipping an earring.

Years later
he chased his youngest son Virgil
around the house,
holding a butcher knife in one hand
and a kitchen chair in the other,
lion-tamer style.
He was babbling about
Indians again, babbling fast
as a flooding creek breaking and foaming
over sharp rocks.

After that
his sons had him committed
to the state hospital. From there
it was just that Thorazine shuffle
in his baggy Big Smiths and slippers,
lips still white from windburn,
forehead still white and a shock
of white hair straight up
from decades of wearing
a stiff-billed farmer cap out in the fields.

They tell me his mother was cold-hearted.
In the flu epidemic of 1918,
his father died young.

I don't doubt Grandad lived a hard life,
trying to raise wheat and cattle
and four sons
on a Cherokee Outlet homestead
all the way through Dust Bowl days
into the era of family-farm foreclosures.

On my wall I keep a picture
so I won't remember him just as a cruel man:
in a white dress and turned-up cap,
he is a blue-eyed baby
grinning
on his daddy's lap.

Wedding Photo of My Parents, circa 1952

Not quite centered
between two tall sprays
of gladioli:
a young man, skin tanned
to a copper sheen, black hair,
striped tie, a slight pout of a smile,
carnation pinned
to the broad lapel
of his baggy suit, half-closed
eyes, spit-shined shoes,
on his left hand the glint
of a gold band.

By his side: a girl
glowing moonlike
in satin pumps,
ankle-length white lace.
With one hand she clutches
a small Bible streaming
ribbons, with the other,
her new husband.
Filmy layers of tulle
in her skirt and veil
blur her image
as if she's been frozen
in a double exposure.
Her smile opens wide.
Her eyes know
no questions. She has found
an answer, she believes.

Father's Day

O human race born to fly upward,
wherefore at a little wind dost thou so fall?
Dante, *Purgatorio*

"Humpty Dumpty fell near here"—
the weird words I woke with
this morning, the middle of June,
Father's Day. And the last time
I talked to my dad was
a Christmas Eve phone call,
when his syllables, like the tree lights,
were vibrant, yet each flashing a separate
color, because he finally can't even
form words. Still, he tries
and tries, a string of sounds that say
nothing. And this, after losing
his sight years ago.
Drink by drink, piece by piece,
I've lost him all my life.
But I have old photos
taken when he was still
whole. In the one on my wall—
the Freedom State Bank calendar shot
from 1941—he poses
with his three little brothers:
a row of proud cowboys on the weathered slats
of the cattle-pasture gate.
Western hat, boots, a loosely-held
lariat ready at his bent, blue-jeaned knee.
Open sky and Oklahoma fields
roll out for miles behind them—
short-grass prairie ragged with mesquite,
sagebrush, sunflowers.
And I realize that the line from my dream
has something to do with
this picture, that even in sleep I cannot
rest, but must forever watch
him falling off that fence,
falling to pieces.

Freedom, Oklahoma Rodeo

for Debra Gay Garland

What went on inside
the arena, I'll never know.

As moonlight rolled
across the hoods of rusty pickups
and shiny horse trailers,
my cousin Deb and I,
both thirteen, walked
the red-dirt perimeter, drinking Pepsi
from paper cups, stepping over
manure piles.

Way up in the black sky,
stars shone like pearl snaps
as we skirted stands
full of uncles and aunts, passed
vendors where pink
cotton candy sugared the air, noticing,
with sidelong gazes,
slim-hipped boys in stiff new jeans,
their rhythmic swaggering
in dusty boots.

As we made our giggling rounds,
the announcer's voice bantered
with the clowns,
and every now and then
clomping hooves drew up close behind.

At the level of our blue-shadowed eyes:
muscular thighs in leather chaps
floating past on horseback,
wheat-colored cowboy hats cocked
just right
over eyes that would almost

light on one of us,
then glance off.

All night long
our hearts waited, ready
to explode
like bulls and broncs from their chutes,

the close August air holding us
as if it would never
let go.

Tornado Warning

Around front porches,
neighbors pace.
Women with arms crossed
cautiously press
bare feet to cool cement.
Their husbands
brave out
a few steps
into weed-gnarled lawns.

Chilled
by the sudden stillness,
a young mother
shoos her children
back into the house,
ready herself
to scramble
under a bed,
cheek to unswept dust.

Gray clouds loom
overhead.
Trees stand
motionless.
Telephone wires hang
expectant.

The whole town
is still
as a sketch of a town
done in charcoals.
In a moment
leaves will begin
to stir,
screen doors will slam.

Camp Houston

Midsummer and hot as hell in the farmhouse,
though the water cooler rattled its noisy air
across my grandmother's kitchen, sending
the aroma of fried chicken through all the rooms

and on out the lace-curtained windows.
Even hotter in the pickup, but we'd take any excuse
to go to Camp Houston for chocolate bars, or beef jerky,
or a bag of Fritos, while Grandad fueled the truck.

The Coca-Cola cooler waited, a gleaming red
treasure chest against the back wall. A wave of cold
met your face as you lifted the lid. Slick bottles
of Dr. Pepper, RC Cola, orange and grape soda nested

in a glistening bed of ice. God, that first swig tasted
good. So cold you wanted to hold the bottle against
your flushed cheek, then your sweating forehead.
Next to the cooler, a tall wooden box topped with glass.

A sign above it read *Baby Rattlers*. On tiptoes we cousins
peered in to see the pink and blue plastic baby rattles.
We knew the joke but had to look every time.
Twenty-five years later I bring my husband, two children,

back to see the family farm—acres of canyons
and wheat fields, barbed wire and rattlesnakes.
In the car I silently count years—twenty-two since
my grandfather was committed to the state hospital,

twenty since Grandmother's fatal heart attack,
ten that Dad was lived blind and brain-damaged by booze,
just three since my cousin was found hanging from a necktie
in his city apartment. On Highway 64, just west of Freedom,

we pass White Horse Creek, then Red Horse Creek.
From the highway I see the farm's red-dirt road rolling off

into pastureland and up and over hills like a piece
of Christmas ribbon candy. We drive on.

For miles I think it must be over this hill or the next,
until I finally spot Camp Houston, and we stop for gas.
I urge my children to come in and see the baby rattlers.
They are still there. The kids look, to humor me,

but are not amused. The woman behind the counter
is not that good-hearted-but-rough-around-the-edges one
who used to call my dad Junior when we stopped by back then.
This woman smiles weakly, says there are snakes

in a pit out back if we want to see them.
We walk behind the building, through sun-scorched weeds
crawling with red ants, to a rectangular cement pit.
That familiar dry ticking sound as we step closer.

And deep down in the dark, in heavy coils around
each other, a dozen diamondbacks hiss up at us
from shady corners, flicking their forked tongues,
rattles straight up, fangs ready to strike.

To My First Lover, a Young Auto Mechanic

This morning I woke with
the taste of you
in my mouth,
the familiar smell of motor oil,
Camel cigarettes, and musk cologne
from nights in your Camaro
many years ago.

I've slipped you into
my bed again.

I've watched us
on my parents' icy porch
in the snow-flecked light
of a yard lamp, where we
said goodnight, wrapped around
each other while
the neighborhood slept:
your mouth wet on
my neck, the chill racing
down my back, your articulate
hands beneath
my sweater, mine pleased
at your crotch, the rise
straining against denim,

my body charged
as a souped-up Chevy engine,
your tender blue eyes.

I still dream of us,
a mad tangle of warmth
in the cold, before
it all stopped

like a smashed new car,
still shiny, still tuned for power.

End of August

Tonight, while the half-moon hides
its dark side,
the Siamese tom stretches
black velvet paws,
claws splayed toward a dream:
he hunts, sapphire eyes
focused to sharp points,
all twilight
concentrated in his gaze.
Stealthy as a shadow, he curves
through a creek-bank jungle
of giant ragweed, candelaria,
sunflower stalks.
Yellow mulberry leaves litter the lawn.
From low branches,
bluebirds dive for insects.
Goldfinches search for seeds
in black-eyed Susans.
Baby cottontails munch in tall grass.
Quick eyes everywhere.

To the Pilgrim Bard, in Gratitude

In honor of my great-great grandfather,
the poet Orange Scott Cummins (1846-1928)

I often see you wandering past buffalo wallows, across
black-willow swales, camped under cottonwoods on creek banks,

your mule cart full of bleached bison bones, the air alive
with whippoorwill calls, the ticking whir of rattlesnakes,

wings of wild turkeys rustling in river thickets. I imagine you
writing verse on stripped tree bark, crystallized gypsum,

and flat stones by fitful campfire light. In canyons, on hilltops,
or huddled in your dugout as a Kansas blizzard howls over,

you grip pen and paper with weathered hands under the pale wavering
of a kerosene lamp. In 1871, the Civil War still rattling in your ears,

a photographer's magnesium flare caught that westward slant
in your eye, wide hat-brim circling above long, scout-style curls. Still,

your writing captured more. Poems about ghosts, buffalo herds, Indians,
cowboys, Scots-Irish ancestors, and sodbusters lie buried deep

in your descendants, colorful as the buttes and mesas of the Red Hills
where you settled at last. Fires, floods, family feuds—so much

gets lost. But because we have your words, the wonder holds.
Nothing, not even prairie cyclones, can whisk it all away.

September Moon

Round and yellow as
the eye of that great horned owl
whose call haunts my dreams.

Dust Bowl Diary, 1935

Silt on the dishes.
Rags under the doors.
Horizon coppered by clouds of dirt.
The sun, a dim smear.
No stars, no moon for weeks.
No shadows.

Our farm is sifting away—
only a bit of cornfield stubble
poking up through shifting dunes,
cedars chalked with fine dust,
half-buried fenceposts.

Cattle are dying,
their lungs caked with mud.
Others, blinded by blowing grit,
stumble in brown blizzards.

Once my hair shone like corn silk
under the sun. Now it's dull, dry,
wrapped tight in a bun.

After a while, everything
seems the color of vermin,
the color of moths—
dirty wash pinned to
the clothesline,
damp dishcloths
stretched along windowsills.

This spring, no lilacs;
no luster left in Mother's eyes.

I've forgotten the true
colors of things. Even the sky
turns eerie shades I've never seen.

Tonight, before sleep,
I'll lie still
on dusty sheets,
close my swollen eyelids,
and pray for vivid dreams.

III

Searching for a Spark

Duende

Lorca knew these gusts as spirit,
invisible as wind searching for a spark.
Don't we all want to be set on fire
by a mysterious breath in the dark?
Some call it selling your soul
to the devil: mere mortal one minute,
force of nature the next. We've all
seen it before: van Gogh burning
alive with his wheat fields and starry nights;
Plath pouring out poems in a brilliant fury;
Joplin's voice inhabited by hot, hungry gods;
Hendrix's long, lovely fingers igniting flames.
Hard to know when that breeze might
blow through, the fugitive moment
when someone gets lit, turns to gold.

Another October Night with Van Morrison

1

Notes range and fluctuate: shadows
of geese over cold fields of milo,
a tomcat yowling and gold-eyed under the moon.

2

It isn't so much the darkness, but the light—
nocturnes of gilt and garnet, ruddy Mars regal as Hecate
in sky so clear you notice the colors of stars.

3

These nights I'm awake to the wild:
coyotes yelping in chase, mating calls
of owls, my own lupine dreams.

4

The guttural fire of his song wavers and warms
like candles lit by some young girl pleading with the moon
for a boy with eyes blue as the underside of flame.

5

I'm listening to the thin, curving edge
of something intensely sweet—all the honey
of amber, and all the inclusions.

6

Once more, the season of maple woods, smoked meats,
distilled spirits, and I'm reminded that sometimes
you must open your heart just to discover what comes out.

7

See that one hot star arcing across night,
red sumac firing the hillsides?
Desire remains the final hope, the flame.

Disillusion

Lately I've been channeling dead poets.
I've wrestled angels with Rilke,
mused on moon phases with Yeats,
and this morning—it's Sunday, after all—
I'm visited by my dear Wallace. He brings
news of you. Is it any wonder?
Each day around ten we feel the same
dark encroachment: I dream
of tigers in red weather, you strum
your blue guitar, both of us half asleep
in houses haunted by white gowns and rings.

Santana at Sunset

All day, this December light:
cold to the soul,
mercurial gray, numbing.

Then fading sun
low on the horizon
starts to burn through

as "Oye Como Va" begins,
blazes high and higher.
Clouds shift and glow,

music shimmers. And, finally,
the slow slide—
Carlos fingering "Samba Pa 'Ti."

Oh, everything
softens, echoing
sweet, moaning strings.

Notes held long
on evening breeze
bleed into sky—heartbreaking

blues, smoldering reds—
until I'm in a place
warm enough to imagine

how time's fierce
rhythms could melt
into eternity

while night settles in, black
as thick smoke
from a raging fire.

Sunday

Neighbors drive past piously,
returning home from church,
tires slowly churning snow
to mud.
      They find me odd:
every morning I run
through fields of blinding white
while my two huskies romp
in wild circles around me,
their blue eyes full of God.

Song of the Snake Goddess

I just happen to like apples
and I am not afraid of snakes
                    Ani DiFranco, "Adam and Eve"

The knot of love has come undone
and I have turned you loose.
I've won this game. There you go,
slithering away, silent. Here I stand,
Hecate holding serpents in both hands,
a Minoan snake goddess,
Eve on a good day, strong from eating apples.
Sigmund knew nothing
of women, snakes, and desire.
No woman ever really wants
a snake. They are hardly the stuff of our dreams.
Still, we attract them like charmers.
These reptiles come around, hissing
about bliss, tempting us with forked tongues.
They slide right in
to our lives when we least expect it,
telling sinuous lies, shedding old skins.
I'll never forget the night I found you
in my bed, the chilling venom
of your kiss.

Psychobilly Blues

Right now
we're all white-trash wannabes
as he twirls on a tall, undershot boot heel,
lanky in faded Levi's tight as a drunk's fist
around a frosty bottle of beer.
A nasal twang mellows down to an Elvis drawl,
narrowed eyes hidden in shadow
under the curled felt brim of a sweat-stained,
fifties-style custom cowboy hat.
At a corner table, you're the smoky-eyed woman
who slowly peels the label
from her longneck as he announces
a kinduva psychobilly thang
that goes sumpin' like kis . . .
The honky-tonk piano starts in, and he's off
on a solitary journey, his life-long affair
with the seductress of performing—
all raw talent and stubborn style,
two-day stubble and an overbite
born to sing long and lonesome about
love-gone-wrong, betrayal, and retribution.
Agile fingers play lean, hungry—
foreplay prolonged to near
climax—notes coaxed out of night air, out of
a body bred from Kentucky coal mines
and California dreams. Broken strings flail
as guitar music rages like fire
licked into a frenzy of out-of-control flame.
He chases the dark
with song, pulls sound from far-away
winds and empty rooms until
you are caught
right where you never knew
you wanted to be—
serenaded straight to the pure, primitive place
where your soul just might settle
to divine dust.

Muse

*Poetry will always be
a wild animal.*
William Stafford, *You Must Revise Your Life*

I've seen a wolf
in the woods of a dream.

Her canine contours run
ravenous with color:
sage, pine, sun-yellow,
and canyon-brown, the rich
carnelian of a Mexican sunset.

Lean, leggy,
pink tongue wet and lolling,
she stares me straight in the eye.

Silver moonlight on her back,
wildfire burning in her eyes,
she circles close in the night
daring me.

Janis

She learned to sing in Texas.
That raw fire in her voice came from
there, in gusts and waves,
in Great Plains gales,
gulf heat and stickiness. Listen
to the way some notes seem lifted
by breeze, carried on coastal wind.

Everything's big in Texas—
those bruises she got
in Port Arthur and Austin,
her soul, her song.

She swigged down
Southern Comfort, poured
herself into music,
sang vivid as blood simmering
through a wronged woman's veins.
Finally, she had to go,
and headed for San Francisco,
eating the red sun of rage and sorrow
for breakfast every morning.

She wasn't plain anymore.
Now a wildfire flared
and could be seen for miles—
the kind of prairie blaze
too big to be stopped
that must be allowed
to burn itself out.

Giorgio de Chirico, *The Delights of a Poet*

Witness this lost
hour in autumn:
light swallowed hard,
deep in shadowed portals.

On the horizon, a train leaves
a trail of pale smoke
in cloudless skies.
The searing clock fixes
its stare on a man who walks
away, his long shadow,
a fountain.

The cool noise of water
dances in afternoon air.

Others have seen, under dark
arches, changeless stone,
this exact slant of sun, carried it away.

They too are ruled by time.

Art History Class

By bus,
the older ladies come
to an evening class at the university.
Rows of silver-blue heads
and sweatered shoulders fill
twelve center-most seats.
As they listen to a lecturer
talk of tombs excavated beneath
the floor of St. Peter's in Rome,
stagnant perfume settles
in the room. After slides
and scholarly descriptions of
sarcophagi, ash chests, bodies
placed in shrines and under
slabs, cremations, inhumations,
and urns, thin whispers
speak of bridge and canasta,
how many tables there were,
will be.

Arnold Böcklin, *The Island of the Dead*

Where are we?

Almost dark, the last
amethyst light of evening turns
its back on the colors

we depend on. We are left
in a murky place, floating

toward shadows of cypresses.
Huge rocks rise
shoulder-like from the sea.

We coast in.

The oars turn slow circles—
the only sound—
as we glide
into deep black

where no one waits for us.

Grande Odalisque
in the Louvre

One calm eye
gazes in disdain
at passing visitors
as she leans
on a pale elbow,
lounges on
plump pillows
and sheets of
Persian silk—
blue-green, liquid
as the Mediterranean.
The full moon
of a breast peeks
from beneath
an outstretched arm.
Near one bare
foot: a slender
brass pipe. She pulls
a bed curtain
to her opaline thigh.
Her S-curved
body reclines long,
naked
as a lover's stare.

Georgia O'Keeffe Muses While Painting a
Red Canna: A Rhapsody

In the deep center, red and glowing, a slow burn
spreading, an undercurrent running strong,
the loud ring of a hammer striking
something hard. So alive I could crack
at any moment. So much like reaching to all
creation. What lies beyond the flame, beyond
my grasp? The world seems to be on wheels, going
so fast I can't see the spokes. Something wonderful
about the bigness, and the loneliness, and the windiness
of it all, the beauty of that wild world. I want live people
to take hold of, music that makes holes
in the sky, to love as hard as I can. I want
to go deeper and deeper into my own unknown.
Nobody else has the energy I have. No one else
can keep up. A thing I don't want to hurry is growing
in my brain, my heart, all of me. That spark, that fire
makes life worthwhile, makes me want to go after
everything in the world, want everything
in the world—good and bad, bitter and sweet. I want
it all. And a lot of it too. Yes, I am living.
How could I help it? Balancing on the edge
of loving like I imagine we never love but once.

Acknowledgments

Grateful acknowledgment is made to the editors of the following publications in which individual poems or earlier versions of them first appeared:

Blue Unicorn
Concho River Review
Cottonwood
Earthwise Poetry Review
Kansas City Star
Kansas City Voices
Kansas Voices
Kansas Women Writers
Lawrence Journal-World
The Louisville Review
The Lucid Stone
The Midwest Quarterly
Owen Wister Review
The Pawn Review
Phoenix Papers: 26 Lawrence Poets
Plainsongs
Potpourri
Riverrun
The Same
Santa Fe Literary Review
West Branch
Westview

Thanks to Michael L. Johnson, Denise Low, Elizabeth Shultz, and Kevin Rabas, for their editorial suggestions and encouragement. And many thanks to Louis Copt for offering the image of his beautiful painting *Legacy of Light* for the cover.